KING HENRY IV

PART I

NOTES

including
Scene by Scene Synopsis—Character Sketches
Selected Examination Questions and Answers

Cliff's Notes
INCORPORATED
BETHANY STATION • LINCOLN 5, NEBRASKA

INDEX

INTRODUCTION

King Henry IV (Part I) was probably written in 1597 and produced in 1598. There were five publications of the play during Shakespeare's lifetime, and, along with Hamlet and Othello, it is one of Shakespeare's three most popular plays.

The play is one of a series of historical plays dealing with the seating of the Lancastrian line on the throne of England. Richard II, which tells the story of the last of the Yorkist kings, is really an introduction to King Henry IV. Whereas Richard II is a study in bad kingship, King Henry IV (both parts I and II) emphasize the growth of young Prince Hal toward the ideal kingship which is exemplified in the play and the man King Henry V. Henry IV himself is not an ideal king, but he is a conscientious king and wants his son to ready himself for the crown. Prince Hal's surface unwillingness to prepare himself for kingship worried Henry IV, and Henry considered the possibility that Prince Hal's madcap pranks were God's punishment to Henry IV for overthrowing Richard II.

The main plot of the play follows rather closely the historical facts set forth by English historian Holinshed in his Chronicles of England, Scotland, and Ireland (1577). Naturally, Shakespeare invented the inimitable characterizations himself. One deviation from fact is Shakespeare's making Hotspur and Prince Hal the same age; historically, Hotspur was much older than Prince Hal. This change, of course, heightens the effect of the drama by establishing Hotspur, whose name so well describes him, as the perfect foil to the character of Prince Hal—another triumph in artistry for Shakespeare.

The comic relief in the play is supplied by Prince Hal and his lusty companion Falstaff in a very powerful sub-plot. The chief source for the comedy elements is a crude play called The Famous Victories of Henry the Fifth, which was issued in England in 1594. Although Falstaff was probably named for a historical character, Sir John Fastolfe, he was based primarily upon a character called

Sir John Oldcastle in the above-mentioned play. But only in Shakespeare's play does Falstaff flower into a full, life-breathing comic character.

Briefly, the historical background for the play is this. In the late fourteenth century King Richard II had unjustly seized the estates of Bolingbroke (later King Henry IV) after the death of Bolingbroke's father, who was Richard's uncle. Henry was exiled to France but returned to England while Richard was in Ireland. Henry aroused an army of friends and threatened Richard, who abdicated the throne. Later Henry ordered the murder of Richard and ascended to England's throne himself. Henry, then, was a usurper of the throne, and, in Shakespeare's play, he was disturbed about that, even though Richard II was a tyrant and deserved to be overthrown.

The conflict between King Henry IV and the Percy family (the Earl of Worcester, the Earl of Northumberland, and Hotspur) provides the plot center of the play. The Percys helped Henry to the throne, but they resented Henry's imperious actions after he became king. Henry and the Percys quarreled; the Percys then tried to stir up a rebellion against the king. The story of the play is the gathering of this rebellion up to the Percy's defeat at Shrewsbury.

The central theme of the play seems to be a plea for unity and order. *King Henry IV (Part I)* exhibits the evils that come to a realm through civil war and disorder. A subsidiary theme, like the subsidiary plot, almost received more emphasis than the main theme. The preparation of Prince Hal for the kingship is the subsidiary theme, and thorough reading of the play reveals a rather solid Prince Hal beneath the surface Hal, who *seems* the playboy type before he becomes king. Proof of the Prince's kingly potential appears in his closing speech, Act I, Scene 2:

"So, when this loose behaviour I throw off...
...And like bright metal on a sullen ground,
My reformation, glittering o'er my fault,
Shall show more goodly and attract more eyes
Than that which hath no foil to set it off.
I'll so offend, to make offence a skill;
Redeeming time when men think least I will."

As Shakespeare matures in playwriting, he tends to use prose more and more. In *Henry IV (Part I)* the prose, especially in the Falstaff scenes, is more important than in any of Shakespeare's plays written or produced up to this time. The play, then, offers the audience a great experience in the theatre — significant actions, worthy themes, vigorous characterizations, and brilliant, appropriate style. No wonder that *Henry IV* received instant and widespread acclaim. Its popularity has continued to the present day, though the roles of both Prince Hal and Falstaff are difficult to fill.

ACT I, SCENE 1

SYNOPSIS

The scene gives the political setting of the play. King Henry is holding a meeting of part of his council at which are present his son Prince John, the Earl of Westmoreland, Sir Walter Blunt and other members. The Prince of Wales is not present. We learn why later. The King says that after the bloody broils, both foreign and domestic which have plagued the last year, now that everything is peaceful he intends to carry out his old intention of leading a crusade to the Holy Land and asks Westmoreland, who has been left in charge of arrangements, to report what action the council took the day before. Westmoreland replies that Edmund Mortimer, Earl of March, in charge of defense on the Welsh borders has been defeated in a bloody battle and captured. Also that there has been an invasion of the north of England by a Scottish army but that he has not received word of the outcome, although a battle was in progress when the messenger left.

King Henry himself has received later news by Sir Walter Blunt, which is that Henry Hotspur, son of the Earl of Northumberland, has stopped the invasion, beaten the Scots and captured many prisoners, among them several Earls of whom the most important is the Earl of Douglas. He has also heard that Hotspur refuses to send the King any of the prisoners but the Earl of Fiffe. The Earl of Westmoreland says that this must be the advice of the Earl of Worcester, brother to Northumberland, who hates the King.

The King has summoned the Earl of Worcester and Northumberland with Hotspur to explain this action and summons the council for the next Wednesday at Windsor. He sadly admits that he must give up his plans for the Holy Land temporarily.

CHARACTERS IN SCENE 1

King Henry

He has a regal dignity of bearing and speech, is quick and decisive in action, shows instant grasp of the situation and is bold. He displays also an underlying religious feeling in his resolve to go on a crusade. His words concerning Hotspur are full of generous admiration, partly prompted by his chagrin at the wildness and apparent dissoluteness of his own son Henry, Prince of Wales.

The Earl of Westmoreland

Brother-in-law of the King, he is his loyal executive, though actually his part is slight.

Sir Walter Blunt

He is present during the scene but does not speak; only the King and Westmoreland do that. He has just acted as messenger bringing the latest news of the battle of Homildon Hill.

Other Characters

The following characters are mentioned but do not appear in this scene:

The Earl of Northumberland

Warden of the Scottish border, he appears mainly as Henry Hotspur's father. He is aging and leaves the main work of the border defense to his son.

Henry Hotspur

He is mentioned in glowing terms by the King as an intrepid leader in battle and famous, though the King has no intention of humoring his pride and insubordination in the matter of the Scottish prisoners.

The Earl of Douglas

Warden of the southern border of Scotland and therefore the Earl of Northumberland's opposite, he belongs to an ancient and famous family. He had taken the opportunity of unsettled conditions in England after Henry IV's accession to the throne to organize a formidable incursion but was defeated by Hotspur's leadership.

Mortimer, Earl of March

Through his grandmother Philippa he is the great-grandson of Edward the Third. Because his line is senior to that of Henry IV his claim to the throne is better than Henry's and he had been designated as the heir by Richard II. There was no objection to claiming the throne of England through the female line, if one could enforce that claim. Edmund Mortimer was not the man to enforce it. Appointed Warden of the Welsh marshes he has been defeated in a bloody battle by Owen Glendower, a rebel leader leading a Welsh insurrection, and has been taken prisoner.

Glendower

Rather a remarkable Welshman educated at the English court, he had returned to his own people to lead a movement for independence. He had remarkable success at first and in this scene has just defeated the Earl of March leading a west-of-England army.

PURPOSE OF SCENE 1

1. To give the political setting of the play, explaining the general situation to the audience. It does this with remarkable economy of time and words, yet manages to maintain a free political level.

2. To introduce the King as one of the chief characters by his presence, and other chief characters by mention.

3. To prepare the audience for Scene 2 showing Henry, Prince of Wales, amongst his low companions.

4. To prepare for Scene 3 when Hotspur and his father and uncle appear before the King in council.

5. To strike the imagination of the audience immediately and gain instant attention by the pageantry of a royal council. The English people were even more susceptible to pageantry then than now.

SUGGESTED QUESTIONS

1. In line 40 what does Westmoreland mean by, "the irregular and wild Glendower?"

2. In line 87 what is the King's reference in the words, "That some bright tripping fairy had exchanged in cradle-clothes our children?"

3. In line 98 what does Westmoreland mean by the words, "and bristle up the crest of youth?"

ACT I, SCENE 2

SYNOPSIS

This scene is purposely a violent contrast with the preceding one which expressed dignity and high formality. Here we have nothing serious, but engaging flippancy and badinage and the endless punning of Falstaff, the greatest comic character of English and, perhaps, any other literature. The change from the blank verse of Scene 1 to the racy prose of Scene 2 fits and heightens the difference of mood.

As the scene opens, the Prince and Falstaff are ribbing each other brightly in an apartment of the Prince's in London. We are introduced to Falstaff's genial humor and nimble wit, and to the Prince's lesser wit with its easily felt background of good sense. A fair part of Falstaff's humor consists in punning (a popular accomplishment in Shakespeare's day though somewhat fallen into disfavor in our day): three uses of the word "grace"; squires of the night's body for Knight's body; thieves of the day's beauty for day's booty; under whose countenance we steal for under whose moral support as well as under whose face.

The Prince reminds Falstaff of the uselessness of stealing purses only to carouse with them and rise as high as the gallows. Whereupon Falstaff changes the subject and the Prince follows with another nonsensical change of subject about a buff jerkin. And then we find out that the Prince has been paying for all of Falstaff's drinks.

Falstaff is obsessed with this idea of the gallows and suggests he do away with them when he becomes king. When Falstaff finds that the Prince did not mean that he would make him a judge, but the hangman, he is just as well suited, for if he does not hear suits in court, meaning cases, he will obtain suits, for it is the hangman's privilege to claim the clothes of the man he has hanged.

Poins comes in with the news that the others have made an arrangement to rob some pilgrims and traders at Gadshill early the next morning. Falstaff suggests the Prince make one of the party. He refuses until Poins persuades Falstaff to leave and explains to the Prince that it's his plan to have a joke on the others and especially Falstaff. They will let the other four rob the travellers and then they will rob the others just to hear Falstaff's story, his wild exaggerations when they meet for dinner in Eastcheap. The Prince is tickled and consents to go with Poins for the fun of it. Poins leaves and, in the first soliloquy of the play, the Prince explains to himself that he is not corrupted but can cut away from this fun he is having when he pleases and he will some day soon.

CHARACTERS IN SCENE 2

Prince Hal

Behind his banter and his delight in baiting the irrepressible, brilliantly resilient Falstaff there is noticeable a good sense and a balance. He does take part in the robbery after refusing to do so, in order to have a bit of fun with Falstaff afterward. However, even if he means to return the money, he has made himself an accessory by knowing of the plotting of the robbery and doing nothing to prevent it. Perhaps, the Elizabethan and the Lancastrian conscience in such matters was a little coarser than that of our time, and a joke would excuse much.

He has been accused of snobbery and sophistry in his soliloquy. Sophistry there is, especially in the last two lines, but no snobbery. He is perfectly well aware of the character of his companions but holds with them because of his delight in Falstaff and his friendship for Poins. It must be remembered that he is excusing himself to his conscience after his escapades, not planning a life of such escapades beforehand. This largely excuses the sentiment of those last two lines but not quite. It is clear that he does not intend to break with these companions, at least not yet, and he must have some high-sounding excuse to silence that conscience. He does reveal a sense of his responsibilities, of his high calling, and he reveals a high purpose which he postpones for the moment.

Falstaff

Behind his wit there lies a stock of good sense and that is one thing that endears him to the Prince. He is a compound of the most opposite characteristics. He boasts and lies but he is neither boaster nor liar because we feel that he does not take himself or anything he says too seriously and does not expect anyone else to do so either. It is all part of a delightful game, an act which he is staging every minute of the day. Never at a loss for a reply or repartee, his quips are never labored; it is all effortless and natural. Rascal he may be, but a genial one because he does not take his rascality seriously, and really stands above it.

Poins

He is obviously closer to the Prince than Falstaff, though he is obviously more or less a professional thief. He is more of the born gentleman than Falstaff but infinitely inferior in all qualities which are great in Falstaff. There is a reference to Henry IV, Part II, to the Prince's having been intimate with Poins' sister, but obviously the Prince likes him for himself too.

PURPOSE OF SCENE 2

1. This scene introduces the subplot, with Falstaff dominating it as he dominates all the rest of the play.

2. It provides a violent contrast of mood and action which raises the audience's interest to a high pitch, holding it breathless.

3. It prepares for Act II, Scenes 1 and 2, and the joke on Falstaff.

4. It puts the audience at ease about the real character of Prince Hal.

SUGGESTED QUESTIONS

1. In line 15, what does Falstaff mean by, "grace thou wilt have none"?

2. What does he mean in line 19 by, "prologue to an egg and butter"?

3. In line 42 why does Prince Hal mention "a buff jerkin"?

4. In line 84 what does Falstaff mean by, "I would to God thou and I knew where a commodity of good names were to be bought"?

ACT I, SCENE 3

SYNOPSIS

At the council meeting called by the King in Scene 1, the King confronts the three Percys. He peremptorily accuses them of contumacy and insubordination. The Earl of Worcester reminds him of the Percy's help when he was seeking the throne and suggests ingratitude. The King flares up, accuses him of "insolence" and orders him to leave forthwith. After Worcester's departure, Northumberland tries to make out that Hotspur's refusal of the Scottish prisoners has been misinterpreted to the King. Hotspur then launches into a lengthy vindication of his actions, saying that just after the battle a court fop from London arrived and angered him so much by his effeminate behavior that he answered him in anger he knows not what, but that he did not deny the prisoners to the King. The sensible Sir Walter Blunt interposes to suggest to the King that whatever Hotspur said at the time may reasonably be allowed to die if he delivers the prisoners now. The King replies that Hotspur still denied the prisoners unless the King will ransom Mortimer, who is Hotspur's brother-in-law, from captivity with Owen Glendower. He accuses Mortimer of having wilfully betrayed his trust and his men, and says that one proof of this is that he has married Glendower's daughter. He flatly refuses to ransom a traitor. Hotspur then springs to Mortimer's defense in hot and angry words, saying that he fought an epic duel with Glendower on the banks of the Severn. This last the King categorically denies, gives the Percys permission to go home and send him the Scottish prisoners on pain of severe punishment, and leaves the room.

Left alone, Hotspur heatedly declares to his father he never will send the prisoners. Worcester comes back and Hotspur goes off into a series of lengthy tirades against the King, while Worcester and his father both try to calm him down. Finally Worcester manages to get a word in and tells of a plot that is already in the making for Glendower and Mortimer, the Archbishop of York, Douglas and his Scottish friends, together with the Percys to rise against the King. He tells Hotspur to set his prisoners free without ransom and they will join the plot. Hotspur is delighted with the idea, and the three leave to arrange the details.

CHARACTERS IN SCENE 3

King Henry

He is dominating, not to say overbearing, in his opening speech, but Worcester certainly is insolent in his reply, though this hardly excuses the King for so quickly sending Worcester out of the room like a naughty child. He is on surer ground in his denunciation of Mortimer, Earl of March, because his marriage to the daughter of the rebel leader Owen Glendower, the King's enemy, would certainly indicate treason, if there were no other consideration. Once again the King is domineering and peremptory in this last speech when he threatens the Percys with swift punishment.

Apparently the only thing that can explain the King's attitude is that he knows something of Worcester's plot which is already in process of formation, suspects the other Percys of being a party to it and reasons that the denial of the prisoners and the insistence on the ransoming of Mortimer is just part of the scheme. He forsees that with Mortimer back in England, allied to Glendower with his Welsh rebel armies, the Percys will probably move to set Mortimer on the throne, because legally he has a better right to it. So he will maintain a front which on no account could be mistaken for weakness or fear, sure as he is that he can handle the Percys and Mortimer if they do rise. In this he proves right.

Hotspur

Here we see the initial development of the character of this hot-headed, impatient, vehement and yet imaginative fighter. Impetuous and uncontrolled, he is courteous in spite of his direct, blunt speech. His nature is poetic as well as combative and his worship of honor, his scorn of meanness and his chivalry are his outstanding qualities for which he was famous in his own time as he has been since. He is quick to understand the plot and its implications, but is enthusiastic for it as much because it means his beloved battle-action for himself as for its political significance.

Worcester

Here he justifies Westmoreland's estimate of him as malevolent toward the King. His insolence in his first speech is not in words only but in looks and bearing. He has already a plot against the King in process of formation, and his knowledge of that makes him bolder before the King than he would otherwise be. He is a very fox for intrigue, something which is foreign to Hotspur's nature, and this incident of the prisoners and Mortimer gives him his opportunity of enlisting his fiery nephew as the battle leader of the revolt.

Northumberland

Though his words are comparatively few they are as telling. A man of poise and strong personality, he is a man of judgment also and of worldly wisdom.

CHARACTERS NOT PRESENT BUT MENTIONED

Mortimer

His superior right to the throne of England is explained here, and also that he was acknowledged by Richard II as his heir before Richard left for Ireland in 1399. We learn of his defeat, which is regarded by Henry as incompetence or treachery, and of his marriage to the daughter of Owen Glendower, his captor and Welsh rebel leader. This constitutes treason in Henry's eyes.

Glendower

Welsh rebel leader, who claims powers as a magician, but is also a splendid military leader.

PURPOSE OF SCENE 3

1. This introduces us to the Percy-Glendower-Mortimer-Douglas rising which forms the main plot of the play.

2. We have an explanation of Mortimer's claim to the throne.

3. We see the relationship of the Percys and Mortimer, who is Hotspur's brother-in-law, and we see the strong family feeling between them.

4. To introduce Hotspur's fiery character.

5. To show the domineering character of the King in these early years of his reign.

SUGGESTED QUESTIONS

1. In line 83 why does Henry say, "damned Glendower"?

2. In line 143 what does Hotspur mean by "an eye of death"?

3. In line 208 what does Hotspur mean by, "But out upon this half-faced fellowship"?

4. In line 209 what does Worcester mean by, "He apprehends a world of figures here"?

5. In line 266 what does Worcester mean by, "Shall secretly into the bosom creep"?

ACT II, SCENE 1

SYNOPSIS

Here we are back in the sub-plot, as in Scene 2 which carries on the action of this one. The place is an inn-yard at Rochester on the Canterbury road south-east of London.

Two carriers with lanterns are loading their horses at four in the morning. Their characteristic conversation is an historical document invaluable to us in picturing the common life of the sixteenth century. They mention the Great Dipper in the sky; their concern for their horses; they contrast the present indifferent hostler with his predecessor, Robin, who was honest and decent; they grumble about the fleas that have bitten them all night; they complain of the moldy peas and beans which have been fed to their horses. They mention that their cargo is bacon, turkeys and ginger destined for London.

Gadshill appears, tries to borrow a lantern to discover what their load is, but is rebuffed by the carriers who refuse to lend him one or tell him their route. They go to waken the gentlemen who are going to travel with them for safety.

Gadshill calls the chamberlain, or steward in charge of the rooms, who is obviously a confederate of his of long standing, providing him information about travellers—their routes, destinations, money or goods. Gadshill learns that there is an official of the royal treasury going along carrying three hundred marks (about $5,000). There is considerable rough banter between the two and Gadshill in his self-importance very nearly gives away the fact that the Prince of Wales is to be one of the robbing party. The chamberlain is promised his share and expects it.

CHARACTERS IN SCENE 1

Gadshill

A cock-sure, bluff, professional thief and highwayman, distinctly below the level of Falstaff and Poins. He has a professional arrangement with the chamberlain to keep him informed of worthwhile victims. He relies on Falstaff and Prince Hal to keep him from the gallows and is perhaps hardened to the prospect of that fate anyway. His boasting of great personages who will protect him so that he may "steal as in a castle" serves to keep the audience reminded that the Prince is to be one of this party and keeps up the tension.

The Carriers

Or as we should say, carters, only that they did not have wagons but panniers on the flanks of their horses. Honest, decent, humble folk but alert and wise to the ways of the road. They suspect Gadshill instantly and will neither lend him a lantern nor give him information, though unwittingly they do in the 2nd carrier's last words, "for they have great charge."

The Chamberlain

A common enough type at that day, and certainly not unknown today, who hypocritically appears a perfectly trustworthy employee but is a rogue in league with rogues outside.

PURPOSE OF SCENE 1

1. To prepare the audience for the actual robbery in Scene 2.
2. To appeal mainly to the "pit" by the presentation of the types and the language with which they are familiar.
3. By the realism of this scene, to make the far more difficult following scene seem plausible.
4. Each scene of the sub-plot fills in a space of time between the scenes of the main plot. This one fills in between two scenes presenting two stages of the development of the Percys' rising.

SUGGESTED QUESTIONS

1. What does Gadshill mean in line 48 and 49 by, "than giving direction doth from labouring; thou lay'st the plot how"?

2. "Eggs and butter" is mentioned many times in this play. What would you argue from that?

3. Why does Gadshill call highwaymen, "Saint Nicholas' clerks"?

4. In line 84 what does Gadshill mean by, "we have the receipt of fern-seed"?

ACT II. SCENE 2

SYNOPSIS

On the highway in the dark near Gadshill, Poins and the Prince are hiding, but Poins has hidden Falstaff's horse in the woods and Falstaff, looking for his horse and suspecting Poins, stumbles on them. There is no use trying to hide now so the Prince and Poins talk freely with the others. For once Falstaff is more than half serious. This trick of hiding his horse is really annoying and painful. It is no joke for one of his girth and weight to be stumbling around in the dark over rough ground. Gadshill, Bardolph and Peto join them and then Poins and the Prince leave them to take up a position further down the hill.

The group of travellers arrive and the four who are left have no difficulties in robbing them and binding them. Then they disperse and re-assemble further down the hill to share the booty. Here Poins and the Prince jump out of hiding in the woods, attack them and put them all to flight immediately, except Falstaff who stands his ground for a moment or two and then disappears in all haste into the dark. Poins and the Prince discard their disguises of buckram overalls, take their booty and ride away.

CHARACTERS IN SCENE 2

Prince Hal

He avoids taking part in the actual robbery but carries on with the practical joke on Falstaff. When it is over he is hugely amused.

Falstaff

Even in this scene he does not take himself seriously, though the hiding of his horse is very serious to him. His reference to levers to lift him up, his threat to kill Poins, are as little serious as the rest of his remarks as shows the expression which follows, "and yet I am bewitched with the rogue's company." Even his bloodthirsty shouts at the travellers are sheer exuberant fun to him, "bacon-fed knaves!", "they hate us youth," "hang, ye gorbellied knaves," "young men must live." It's all part of the play he's playing every day, and he can't even be serious when he's taking part in a highway robbery.

Gadshill, Bardolph, Peto

Mere cowards who run without a show of fight.

Poins

He has the sense of humor of a practical joker, and has enough executive ability to carry out his jokes.

PURPOSE OF SCENE 2

1. To show the actual robbery and the practical joke successful.

2. To whet the audience's curiosity about the exaggerated account that Poins and Prince Hal expect from Falstaff.

3. To show Falstaff not taking himself seriously and making jokes about himself even in a highway robbery, and even when he has been put to untold discomfort by the hiding of his horse. To show also that Falstaff is not a coward. One must remember that a man of his bulk and age would be at a hopeless disadvantage against two nimble youths, and he was left to handle them alone.

SUGGESTED QUESTIONS

1. Why is this scene entirely in prose?
2. Why do the travellers appear dismounted on the stage?

ACT II, SCENE 3
SYNOPSIS

The scene is Harry Hotspur's castle of Warkworth in the North of England. Hotspur is striding up and down the room reading a letter by fits and jerks, sentence by sentence, and commenting in fury between each sentence and the next. The letter is from some unnamed person whom he has counted on for support and who is refusing to be drawn into the plot, naming his reasons—their cause is dangerous, the time unsuitable, their friends uncertain, the whole plot too light. Hotspur's fury mounts as he defends the plot aloud— a good plot as ever laid, friends true and constant. He names over the main supporters: his father, his uncle, himself, Mortimer, the Archbishop of York, Owen Glendower and Douglas. Thereupon he launches into a tirade of epithets and names against this faint-hearted friend, "cowardly hind," "lack-brain," "frosty-spirited rogue," "this rascal, I could brain him with my lady's fan," "pagan rascal," "infidel," "dish of skim milk." He ends up by expecting that this person will go to the King and reveal the plot and he defies him to do so, saying that they are prepared.

Lady Percy enters and without a word of endearment he says that he must leave within two hours. She is almost tearful as she asks why she has been utterly neglected by him for the last two weeks, and wants to know what is so preying on his mind that he is silent, nervous, pale and melancholy. In his restless sleep he has been ejaculating murmurs concerning war and naming armament and equipment, talking of ransoms and soldiers killed. She wants to know what it is all about.

Hotspur has not heard her or he ignores her for he does not answer her but calls for his servant and wants to know whether his messenger has gone with the letters and whether his horse has arrived.

When Lady Percy inquires what it is that is carrying him away, he answers in teasing flippancy, his horse.

She answers his flippancy with one of her own; she will break his little finger if he does not tell her all things true.

Undoubtedly he loves her, or he would not be so concerned about her brother Mortimer, and undoubtedly he kisses her, but mockingly follows it up with, "Away, I love thee not, I care not for thee, Kate."

She pouts that if he does not love her, she will not love herself. She knows full well he loves her, but, womanlike and reasonably, she would like a little show of affection now and then, and would like to share his confidence, especially when she guesses by herself the absolute fact, "I fear my brother Mortimer doth stir about his title and hath sent for you to line his enterprise." She gets the instigator wrong, but she is near enough.

Mockingly, teasingly, he tells her he will not confide in her — in other words, he must not tell anyone. However, he is going today, but she will follow him tomorrow, and he holds her at arm's length to watch her face as he asks, "Will this content you, Kate?"

She pouts, "It must of force," meaning she wants really to ride with him.

This is one of the tenderest of Shakespeare's love scenes and utterly different from any other. The rough, impetuous, honor-seeking warrior can mock and tease his doting wife because he knows she can read between his lines; she knows he loves her, and she understands his light-hearted half-serious banter.

CHARACTERS IN SCENE 3

Hotspur

His impatient fiery nature is evident again in his comments on the letter — a very straightforward letter, by the way. It would appear that through his impetuousness, he has made a serious mistake in ever counting on this person and approaching him with his plans. But count on him he has, and it would seem with some reason, for the correspondent opens with the admission, "in respect of the love I bear your house." Each comment of the writer infuriates him further, but finally with swift sober judgment he realizes that this man will probably inform the King. He dismisses him from his mind with, "Hang him! let him tell the King: we are prepared."

His treatment of his wife seems to have been widely misunderstood. It is because he does not want her involved in his plot that he will not tell her about it, not because he thinks little of her. Undoubtedly his arm is about her when she says, "I'll break thy little finger, Harry." Undoubtedly he kissed her there, and immediately afterward pretends to throw her away, but certainly she is in his arms to the end of the scene. He loves her, and knows that she knows it.

Lady Percy

Love and her man are all she cares about. Politics mean nothing to her—even her brother's title to the throne. Not a weak young woman, she is utterly feminine. She understands his apparent roughness to her, his mocking and teasing; his actions belie his words, and there is a certain light-heartedness and gaiety about him when he smells a battle in the offing which she has experienced before and that only recently, no doubt. But she does want desperately to be confided in and to be with her husband. She understands, too, her husband's utter aversion to any love-making which a modern school-boy would call "mushy."

PURPOSE OF SCENE 3

1. To show the leader of the revolt sure that his arrangements are complete and ready for action.

2. By the tone and arguments of the letter to raise some doubts in the audience's mind as to the success of the rising, and so prepare the audience subtly for the eventuality.

3. To show another side of Hotspur's nature by the introduction of Lady Percy.

SUGGESTED QUESTIONS

1. In line 70 what does Hotspur mean by, "O Esperance!"?

2. In lines 92 and 93 explain, "cracked crowns and pass them current too."

3. In line 48 explain, "speak terms of manage to thy bounding steed."

ACT II, SCENE 4

SYNOPSIS

Here we have Falstaff at his very prime and peak. It is perhaps the greatest comic scene in drama, certainly in English drama. Throughout, the inimitable knight speaks hardly a serious word and there only by way of stage-management, for he is staging his daily play, by and with himself. Under his influence Prince Hal, too, speaks very few serious words, for he dearly loves to play opposite this prince of actors, who has the power of turning any human being from Prince Hal to Bardolph or the Hostess into a supporting cast. In Henry IV Part 2 we see that he can turn even the Lord Chief Justice of England, out for his blood, into a supporting cast.

The scene opens with Prince Hal and Poins at the Boar's Head Tavern in Eastcheap. Prince Hal has been amusing himself while waiting for Poins by getting acquainted with the drawers, or as we should say, tapsters, down in the cellars among the hogsheads of wine, and learning their trade jargon or slang. Then, while waiting for the others, the Prince and Poins amust themselves by baiting Francis, one of the apprentice waiters at the inn. Poins goes into a room nearby and keeps up an incessant calling of "Francis!" while the Prince keeps him there asking about his apprenticeship. Francis calls "anon, sir," or as a waiter today would say, "coming, sir," while the Prince asks him another question to keep him there. At last, the Prince runs out of questions and talks pure nonsense to the lad till he doesn't know what he is doing. The vintner finally arrives and puts an end to this nonsense by sending Francis to the guests in another room, and tells the Prince that Falstaff and the others are at the door. The Prince tells him to let them wait awhile and then admit them.

Poins asks the Prince what this baiting of Francis was all about. The Prince replies that it was merely a whim to see if the boy could say anything else but "Anon, Sir." Then he says he is not yet inclined to be as serious and energetic as this Hotspur of the North who kills half a dozen Scots before breakfast, washes his hands and says, "Fie, upon this quiet life! I want work." Then he tells Poins to call in Falstaff and they'll stage a play, the Prince as Hotspur and Falstaff as Lady Percy.

Falstaff and the others come in with Francis behind bringing wine. What follows is Falstaff's masterpiece of foolery. He plays his part so extremely well that he actually takes in Prince Hal and Poins who show that they believe that Falstaff has been serious by their utter anticlimax of telling the straight prosaic story of the event. Falstaff makes one gallant attempt to raise the drooping drama to the stage of splendid make-believe by his foolery of the lion and the true prince. When this fails, as he sees it does, he changes the subject and calls boisterously for a play extempore. To his disappointment Prince Hal tries to revive it on the level of serious fact, making him the butt, and in disgust he says, "Ah, no more of that, Hal, an thou lovest me!", meaning, "You've missed the point and the subject is dead."

That Falstaff is not conscious of raising the numbers of assailants from two to eleven and that he is not doing it for effect is absurd. It is also quite certain that he recognizes the Prince and Poins, if not at the moment, certainly in immediate recollection. This is shown by his very pointed reference, "Two I am sure I have paid, two rogues in buckram suits." He points directly at Prince Hal and Poins and says, "I tell thee what, Hal, if I tell thee a lie—" It is a subtle piece of acting and they don't get it.

The hostess enters to say that a nobleman of the court at the door wishes to speak to the Prince. Falstaff offers to send him packing. The moment he is out of the room the Prince asks Peto and Bardolph their account of the fight. They say that Falstaff hacked his own sword and made them tickle their noses so that they would bleed all over their clothes. Prince Hal takes them seriously indicting Falstaff is actually trying to deceive them and so have most of the critics ever since, but they have missed the point that Falstaff was far too good a showman to neglect the "properties," the stage equipment, of his show.

Falstaff returns to say that Sir John Bracy has been sent by the King to tell Prince Hal to report at court in the morning because Glendower, Mortimer, Northumberland, Hotspur, and Douglas have headed a rising. Falstaff twits Hal in bogey-man fashion, asking if he isn't horribly afraid with three such enemies as Douglas, Hotspur and Glendower after him. When Hal answers, "not a whit," Falstaff says that anyway he will receive a horrible scolding from his father in the morning and that he had better practice an answer. And so the extempore play which Falstaff wanted comes on quite naturally and unforced, and both Falstaff and Prince Henry throw themselves into it for all they have, but Falstaff carries off the honors in such effortless fashion that he is confirmed as a star. This is the climax of the finest comic scene in English drama.

Prince Hal tells Falstaff to impersonate his father, the King, and Falstaff accepts the role with alacrity, choosing a chair for the throne, his dagger for sceptre, and a cushion for crown. He must first have a cup of sack (sherry) to make his eyes look red as from weeping. Then he bids the nobility (Poins, Gadshill, Peto, Bardolph) stand aside, and the Queen (hostess) cease weeping (she is almost beside herself with admiration for his acting) and, mimicking after his own inimitable fashion the dignity of the King, delivers a castigation of his son for his riotous behavior amongst low companions. His style is stilted, an imitation of the antithetic style of Lily, called Euphuism—or rather a travesty of that style. Shakespeare travestied that artificial style in others of his plays, notably in the *Midsummer Nights' Dream*. Falstaff's reproof is a masterpiece of fooling and so is his eulogy of himself which follows, in which he drops that Euphuistic style; enough is enough.

Prince Hal impetuously deposes Falstaff and they change roles. Although the Prince as King indicts Falstaff mercilessly, the latter comes off in triumph with as clever a eulogy of himself as he has given before.

The play is interrupted by a knocking at the door. The hostess, Francis and Bardolph rush out, and immediately Bardolph rushes back to report that the sheriff with a large company of men-at-arms is at the door. Falstaff treats this news as an annoying interruption and insists on playing out the play. The Prince sends Falstaff behind the arras and tells them to call in the sheriff.

The sheriff has with him one of the carriers who was with the party that was robbed. He tells the Prince that Falstaff and the others have been followed to the inn, and the party has been identified by "a gross fat man," and the carrier adds, "as fat as butter." The Prince lies to cover his companions and promises the sheriff that Falstaff shall be produced by dinner time that day and asks the sheriff to withdraw. He does so, remarking that it is two in the morning.

The Prince remarks that Falstaff is as well known as St. Paul's Cathedral, and orders Peto to call him out. He goes to the arras and finds Falstaff fast asleep behind it, and snoring. The Prince orders Peto to search his pockets. "Nothing but papers, my lord," says Peto. They find they are lists of capons and sauce (fattened fowl) and great quantities of sack and a half-penny-worth of bread. So they let him sleep where he is. The Prince is off to court in the morning, where he will make Falstaff a captain of infantry. He knows, he says, that a march of 240 yards will be the death of Falstaff. Saying that the money will be more than made good, the Prince is away for the rest of the night.

There is no doubt that there was a typographical error in the early editions of Shakespeare's plays in the first years of the seventeenth century and that is was Poins instead of Peto who remains with the Prince to face the Sheriff.

Prince Hal

This scene somewhat justifies his indiscretions, and undoubtedly it was meant to do so. We find him getting so easily and well acquainted with the tapsters in the cellars, that, set at ease by his charm of personality, they accept him as one of themselves and teach him all their trade jargon. If there were any official excuse for his consorting with the people he has been consorting with it would be that he is getting to know his people at first hand, and that is what he is doing here. Shakespeare does not forget this, either, in his play *Henry V*, where he has Henry wandering among the tents on the eve of Agincourt.

With Francis he is a little cruel but not seriously so. He is in an irresponsible mood.

Both he and Poins mistake Falstaff's subtle drama for seriousness but give him a wonderful chance to play it out until they spoil it all by insisting on giving a factual account.

He shows up well in the extempore drama, but is no match as an actor for Falstaff.

He is not perturbed at the arrival of Sir John Bracy or of the Sheriff; his rank protects him, and he virtually arrogates to himself the sheriff's authority.

Falstaff

Here he is at the top of his form, and inimitable then and now. We have known such people, but not in such quality and such superlative degree. He knows what is expected of him and he gives good measure, pressed down and running over. Like the actor he is he struts in, ignoring the rest who do not yet know that they are going to be his supporting cast and never really find it out. He mutters about cowards, finds the wine adulterated, breaks out loudly about cowards and eulogizes himself. Then he faces around and directly accuses the Prince and Poins of being cowards. When Poins is nettled to the point of talking of stabbing, he is certain. He may not have been quite sure before, but now he knows that it was Prince Hal and Poins who attacked the four and seized the loot. He was prepared for that. There has been no thought before of their running away. The six had been together that morning at four in the darkness. The Prince and Poins had separated to stand lower down the hill. The robbery had been successful. When the four assembled to share the loot they had been attacked — and by whom? Two rogues in buckram. Buckram — the overalls that Poins had provided. If Falstaff could recognize buckram in that darkness he could certainly recognize the Prince and Poins, and, besides, he stayed fighting there long enough to get a closer view.

He faces them and points his sword straight at Prince Hal. "I tell thee what, Hal, if I tell thee a lie, spit in my face." Then he immediately raises the ante to four. Now, that takes the whole little drama out of reality into fantasy where he wants to keep it — if he can keep his extempore cast with him. And for a considerable time they tag along behind him, giving him the center of the stage he needs. He has a sense of proportion, but that does not prevent him from adding a variation of "three misbegotten knaves in Kendal green came at my back and let drive at me; for it was so dark, Hal, that thou coulds't not see thy hand." The Prince takes him up on this point of darkness and being able to distinguish Kendal green, not realizing the pure foolery of it. Seeing the hopelessness of answering such a factual prosaic question which would tear his make-believe to pieces, he immediately shifts his drama to another plane to save it. This is always his nimble practice when he sees his supporting cast getting out of hand or lagging far behind him.

This scene clears up the question of his cowardice. It is he who is ready to face the nobleman from the court and send him packing. The arrival of the sheriff with his men-at-arms does not perturb him. To him it is only an annoying interruption and he insists the play be played out and actually attempts to carry on with it. Then when he is behind the arras he can hear every word the sheriff says. He must hear the first few words at least and knows that it is himself the sheriff has come for; yet he goes peacefully to sleep.

Poins

He joins with the Prince in baiting Falstaff, little realizing that he is one of the supporting cast, but twice he gives Falstaff his chance to lift the drama to the stage again, once in line 236 where he says, "Come, your reason, Jack, your reason," and in line 265 where he says, "Come, let's hear, Jack; what trick hast thou now?" For the rest he simply follows Prince Hal. He shows a hasty and very prosaic temper when he talks of stabbing Falstaff if he calls him coward. The Prince himself does not take it seriously.

Bardolph

He makes a virtue out of the fiery red carbuncles on his nose and cheeks, the result of ceaseless drinking. Prince Henry explains them as a permanent blush of shame from the time when he was caught stealing a cup of sherry eighteen years before. Bardolph says that if one only knew, they mean anger (choler). This gives the Prince a chance to make a pun on the word choler (collar). He is scared stiff when the sheriff arrives and hides with the rest, though he does wait long enough to warn the Prince.

Peto

He explains Falstaff's hacking of his sword with his dagger. The reason that it is supposed that there is a typographical error in leaving Peto with the Prince when all the rest hide is that when the Prince says good night, he says, "Be with me betimes in the morning." Nowhere else is there a suggestion that Peto is on terms of such intimacy with the Prince that he should ask him to come to his rooms early in the morning, and we know that Poins is on just such terms of intimacy. Also, the Prince promises as to the army, "Thy place shall be honourable."

PURPOSE OF SCENE 4

1. To advance the sub-plot to its climax.

2. To carry on the humorous interval between the serious scenes of the main plot as all the scenes of the sub-plot do.

3. To bring the audience up to date on the stage the Percys' plot has reached.

4. To show the rising looked at from the other side.

5. To prepare the audience for both Prince Henry's and Falstaff's parts in the miltary action that follows.

SUGGESTED QUESTIONS

1. In Prince Henry's description of his time with the drawers in the cellar, he quotes one of them as calling out, "Score a pint of bastard in the Half-Moon," What does this phrase mean?

2. There are several oblique references to the Puritans in this scene. Find two of them.

3. What is the hostess' attitude to Falstaff in this scene?

4. What does the word "halter" refer to in line 325?

5. In line 340 what should we use instead of the word "blue-caps"? What figure of seech is this, in which an object is named by an accompanying characteristic?

ACT III, SCENE 1

SYNOPSIS

The heads of the rising, Hotspur, Glendower, Mortimer and Worcester, are holding conference in the Archdeacon's house at Bangor in the far northwest corner of Wales. They have finished their arrangements and now are about to partition England and Wales in three parts. Glendower, wishing to be complimentary to Hotspur, says that King Henry, whenever he speaks of him, turns pale and wishes him in heaven. Hotspur replies that the King wishes Glendower in hell whenever he hears his name. This excites Glendower to boast of the portents which appeared in nature at his birth.

Hotspur rudely ridicules all this as nonsense, and makes Glendower furious. He goes on to boast of his powers of magic which Hotspur ridicules also, and even more scornfully. Mortimer, as chairman of the meeting, tries to keep the peace by calling Hotspur off. He says that Hotspur will make his father-in-law mad. This has no effect on Hotspur, who continues to ridicule Glendower's pretensions, till Glendower, seein he is not impressing Hotspur, gives it up and turns to the map.

Mortimer explains that the Archdeacon of Bangor has divided the country "very equally," by which he means as equally as possible. All west of the Severn shall be Glendower's kingdom, all north of the Trent shall be the Percys', and all south and east of the Trent and the Severn shall be Mortimer's. He goes on to say that the copies of the agreement are being drawn up and may be signed this night. Tomorrow Hotspur, Worcester and himself will move their armies to Shrewsbury to meet Douglas and Northumberland. Glendower will not have his forces assembled for two weeks. Glendower interposes to say that it will not take that long and that he will bring Hotspur's and Mortimer's wives with him.

Hotspur, who has been studying the map and has heard nothing since Mortimer mentioned the Percy assignment, now breaks in to say that his portion is decidedly smaller than either of the other two, that the bend of the river Trent on both sides of the city of Burton-on-Trent cuts into his territory severely. He will have a new channel dug so that the river will run in an even curve and recover a large section of land for him—of course at Mortimer's expense. Mortimer objects, Glendower forbids it, but Worcester backs up Hotspur. It looks as though there is going to be a genuine split amongst the leaders when suddenly Glendower yields and says, "Come, you shall have Trent turned." Whereupon, Hotspur is pacified as suddenly as he flared up. He does not care, he says; he will give thrice as much land to any deserving friend, but he will not be cheated in a bargain. Glendower goes out to hasten the writing of the agreement and to break to their wives the news of their departure.

As soon as he is gone Mortimer chides Hotspur for his contentious stirring up of his father-in-law, Glendower. Hotspur excuses himself on the count of Glendower's tediousness. His chit-chat about the miraculous in early Welsh history bores him to tears. Mortimer excuses and praises his father-in-law and says no other man could have baited him as he has done. Worcester interposes to take Hotspur to task for his manners. Hotspur accepts the reproof meekly with the words, "Well, I am schooled."

Glendower brings in Lady Percy and Mortimer's wife, Lady March. Mortimer is irritated that he can speak no Welsh and she can speak no English, but they are madly in love anyway. She sits down on the rushes which cover the floor and has him lie down and rest his head in her lap. There he makes derisive comments, while Kate tries to make him keep quiet. She uses just such comments as any high school girl might make today to her boy friend. "Wouldst have thy head broken?" she says. "No," answers Hotspur. "Then be still." The high-school girl would say, "I'll pin your ears back if you don't keep quiet."

Glendower obligingly furnishes music from an unseen source which, he says, hangs in the air three thousand miles from there. Then Glendower's daughter sings. No doubt the song was in Welsh on Shakespeare's stage as it is on ours. Then Hotspur urges Kate to sing. She refuses, saying, "Not mine, in good sooth." He teases her for using such a milk and water oath. He wants her to swear a good mouthfilling oath. He urges her again to sing. She refuses firmly, knowing her husband and his contempt for the accomplishment, though, no doubt, she can sing. Hotspur, suddenly reversing his attitude, approves her refusal to sing, jumps up, saying that, if the copies of the agreement are ready, he'll be on his way. They can come when they like. Mortimer, Glendower and the ladies follow immediately.

CHARACTERS IN SCENE 1

Hotspur
    His unconcealed contempt for Glendower and his magical pretensions and his disregard of Mortimer seem to show him intent on breaking up the alliance, but he is merely trying them out to the

limit to satisfy himself as to where they stand and to show them up. His claim to further territory and his announced intention of altering the course of the river Trent are for the same purpose. When they yield the second time he has thoroughly established his ascendancy over them, as he knows he must if there is to be any unity of action. His attitude toward his wife shows his deep affection for her even through his teasing mockery—"Lady as thou art." He has a contempt for the accomplishment of singing, but he enjoys Glendower's music and is a master of high poetic and imaginative phrases. His uncle's trenchant criticisms he accepts because he recognizes the truth of them. While Worcester admits his greatness, courage and spirit, he accuses him of temper, defect of manners, lack of self-control, pride, haughtiness, obstinacy and disdain.

Glendower

His continual assertion of his magical powers has finally actually convinced himself, though he is not above a little sharp practice now and then to help them out—witness the concealing of his musicians behind perforated walls. His conceit is overwhelming. He regards himself as remarkable as a poet, a harpist, master of English and a general. His son-in-law adds that he is exceedingly well-read, valiant, affable and generous. His mercurial temperament is genuinely Celtic for, as suddenly as he flares up, he drops to the opposite extreme. It cannot be denied that there is a great deal of charm about him and that his facility in poetic expression is equal to Hotspur's. It is his posing and absurd pretensions which nauseate Hotspur.

Mortimer

Chairman of this meeting on account of his right to the throne of England, he is unable to control it or keep order. His sentimental talk and behavior to his wife may be excused from one still on his honeymoon, but they are excessive for a general about to go into action. However, some generals, even in their fifties, fall in love very hard when they fall. The main impression is that he is not of the mettle to be a leader in this desperate expedition or to be a kin.

Worcester

In this scene, he shows himself to advantage. He is concerned to keep the peace among the leaders and to keep the expedition together. He backs Hotspur about the river Trent but without enthusiasm. He does his best work in the diplomatic but sufficiently sharp manner in which he sows up Hotspur to himself.

Lady Percy

Thoroughly attuned to her husband's moods, she enters into each one of them automatically. She knows his contempt for sentimentality and love-making in public and plays up to him in his derisive mimicry. She knows his aversion to singing in public and firmly resists his ironic invitation to sing.

Lady Mortimer

Utterly in love with the handsome young husband with whom she cannot converse, she must needs use only the language of the eyes and embraces. This accounts for some of her sentimentality, but she is the very opposite of Kate. She is the clinging vine type, but utterly spoiled, and insistent on having her own way.

PURPOSE OF SCENE 1

1. It provides in its domestic scene in the latter half an emotional and comic relief between its serious first half and the serious Scene 2 which follows.

2. It creates further doubt in the audience's mind as to the possibility of success for the expedition.

3. It gives the audience an opportunity to assess the main leaders in person.

SUGGESTED QUESTIONS

1. What does Glendower mean in line 49 by, "hold me pace in deep experiments"?

2. What is the meaning of, "indentures tripartite," in line 80?

3. What does Mortimer mean in line 167 by "strange

concealment"?

4. What does Lady Percy mean in line 235 by "governed by humours"?

5. What would have been the result for England if the Percys and Glendower had won and divided it?

ACT III, SCENE 2

SYNOPSIS

Here we have the turning point of the play. As is usual in Shakespeare's plays it is in the middle of Act III. Prince Henry is present, as ordered, to receive his medicine. As the King dismisses his lords-in-waiting, he knows that the crisis of his life has arrived.

The King begins by telling the Prince that God must be punishing him for his misdeeds by giving him such a son, one who stoops to such low companions and conduct as he does. The Prince acknowledges his guilt but pleads that his offenses have been exaggerated by newsmongers, who hoped for advantage by tale-bearing. He begs for pardon with this confession.

The King says that he must ask God for the pardon. He ignores the plea of exaggerated reports and wonders how Hal could be so untrue to his descent and heritage as to lose his place in the council to his younger brother. A prince who hopes to succeed to the throne must keep the respect of his future subjects and not make himself cheap in the public eye. He himself had withheld his person from the public gaze except upon important occasions so that his emergence in public was an event. Richard II had made himself so common a sight and behaved so familiarly to everybody that people lost that sense of the exalted in their king and with it their respect. Hal is in much the same position at this moment. He himself is the only person left who is not surfeited with the sight of him.

Hal promises to be himself in the future. The King is not satisfied with this and continues the castigation.

He holds up Hotspur as a shining example of what Hal might have been and ought to be. Of the same age, he had won renown throughout the world. Thrice has he conquered the great Douglas and once made him prisoner, and now made a friend of him. He is leading to battle mature lords and revered bishops. The King insinuates that Hal is an enemy of his, too, and might even take service under Hotspur.

This cuts Hal to the heart. He promises to redeem his misbehavior by personal action in battle against this very Hotspur and to take his honors from him and wear them himself. Of course, he can never do this, for alive or dead, Hotspur's honors and fame will forever be his own. But in the fervent, even desperate, desire of the moment to convince his father of his sincerity, he uses this excited language.

The King, convinced, says that his relief is very great, and that he will give him a command in the army.

Sir Walter Blunt enters and in evident alarm, gives news that the rebel armies have met at Shrewsbury and that they have a formidable array. The King shows his command of the situation by remarking that he has known this for the past five days. He tells Hal that the Earl of Westmoreland has left with his army today for Bridgenorth, which is the royal assembly point, and Prince John has gone with him. Hal will lead his force there next Wednesday and the King himself will go on Thursday.

CHARACTERS IN SCENE 2

King Henry

His dealing with the Prince is a masterpiece of applied psychology and calculated management. He begins on the note of wounded affection, intending to wring Hal's heart, continues on the note of disloyalty to his ancestral heritage, then lost opportunity, then insecurity, and finally damaging comparison. It works, and when he is convinced it has, he gives his full forgiveness without further ado. His religious attitude is evident once more in his words, "God pardon thee," bidding Hal look there and not to him for pardon. Also he shows that he has examined his conscience concerning his treatment of Richard II and his murder and is under no illusion regarding his son in the matter.

He shows that he is fully informed and is in control of the situation regarding the rebels. He has taken all the necessary steps.

Prince Hal
He shows respect and great self-control until his excited last speech which is a desperate last attempt to make his father believe him. He has dignity and restraint, and realizes how precarious his position is with regard to his father's trust until he can show his sincerity in deeds instead of mere words.

Sir Walter Blunt
Once more a messenger, though this time his news is stale.

PURPOSE OF SCENE 2

1. To bring to a climax the main plot by the reconciliation of the King and the Prince of Wales.

2. To keep the audience informed of the progress of events in the war.

3. To show Henry's philosophy of life and his methods of seizing the throne from Richard II.

4. To give a glimpse of the essential Hal.

SUGGESTED QUESTIONS

1. What does the King mean in line 50 by, "And then I stole all courtesy from heaven"?

2. What does he mean in line 69 by, "Enfeoffed himself to

popularity"?

3. What does he mean by line 103, "And, being no more in debt to years than thou"?

4. What does the Prince mean by line 147, "Percy is but my factor"?

ACT III, SCENE 3

SYNOPSIS

When Falstaff does not feel like looking for a supporting cast he wll do a monologue, but he must have an audience and for this Bardolph will do for the moment. He does his monologue on a theme of mock self-pity for his misspent life. Bardolph ventures into the role of supporting cast by telling him he certainly cannot live long. Thus encouraged, Falstaff really goes to work on a mock appreciation of his mock virtes. Then Bardolph has the temerity to mention his enormous girth. Too bad for Bardolph! He's right in the supporting cast now. Falstaff turns upon him and verbally falls upon his blazing nose and cheeks till Bardolph has had enough and to spare. He is saved by the arrival of a new member of the supporting cast, the Hostess of the Inn, who is immediately enrolled. Falstaff is having the time of his life playing cat and mouse with this woman who he knows is fascinated by him, as we have seen in the extempore play scene, and as we judge in this scene by the recital of what she has done for him in the past. He speaks hardly a serious word throughout the whole scene. He knows perfectly well that there was nothing in his pockets but unpaid tavern bills and he knows that everyone else knows this, too. He doesn't expect anyone to believe anything else. But he must play out his little play for all the fun there is in it. The mention of the ring is the peak of the foolery. Everybody in the place knows that ring; everybody knows it is copper as well as Falstaff does, but he manages to make it the climax of his drama till he has the poor woman mentally running around in circles.

The Prince and Poins arrive in half armor doing a military march for comic effect. Falstaff catches the spirit immediately and meets them playing on his walking stick as on a fife to complete the comic effect. The Hostess starts to complain to the Prince about Fastaff but Falstaff takes the story away from her and tells of his pocket being picked and the ring. The hostess accuses him, to the Prince, of slandering even him behind his back and saying that the Prince owed him a thousand pounds. This is the very breath of the drama to Falstaff. The Prince asks, "Do I owe you a thousand pounds?" His repartee is swift, "A million; thy love is worth a million; thou owest me thy love." There is no cornering an extempore actor like that. The Prince confesses that he picked Falstaff's pocket and shows him what he found. Falstaff turns it into a magnanimous gesture of foolery to the Hostess. "I forgive thee; go, make ready breakfast; love thy husband, look to thy servants, cherish thy guests; thou shalt find me tractable to any honest reason; thou seest I am pacified still. Nay, prithee be gone." And go she does.

The Prince tells Falstaff that the money is paid back to the men who were robbed; he is good friends with his father and may do anything. "Rob me the exchequer the first thing thou doest, and do it with unwash'd hands, too." In other words, don't even wait to wash your hands—typically Falstaffian, as the Prince appreciates. The Prince tells him, to his temporary disappointment, that he has procured him the captaincy of a company of infantry and that he is to report at the Temple the next afternoon to receive money and orders for his men's supplies. The Prince is using some of his old acquaintances at the Inn in the army, for he sends Bardolph with letters to Westmoreland and Prince John, whom we know are on their way to Bridgenorth. When the Prince leaves, Falstaff calls loudly for his breakfast, and sighs that he wishes he could make the Inn his headquarters.

CHARACTERS IN SCENE 3

Prince Hal

In spite of his promises to his father and his firm intentions, he is not the type to desert promptly or curtly his old acquaintances with whom he has had so much fun, disreputable as they may appear. He returns to the Inn to enlist them in the war effort. He thoroughly appreciates the drama which he finds in progress and immediately becomes one of the supporting cast, giving Falstaff at least three opportunities for magnificent repartee—the one about "a million"; the one about Adam and the state of innocency; and the address of reconciliation to the Hostess. He is serious in purpose but still the same fun-loving Hal.

Falstaff

Still playing his daily play to himself, he becomes serious only for a second when he finds his command is to be in the infantry. His character in this scene has been treated in the above synopsis.

Bardolph

He has a certain sense of humor and that is no doubt why Falstaff takes such delight in his company, and the Prince employs him. His first speech is a very sly dig. He is, we find, somewhat sensitive about his face, but his remark about the marching when the Prince comes in shows his appreciation of essential fact. "Yea, two and two, Newgate fashion."

Poins

There is a real difficulty here. There seems to have been some carelessness in preparing the first editions of Shakespeare's plays for the press. The acting editor may have used either Poins' or Peto's names at different times and the change was not completely carried through by the publisher. At any rate, all the internal evidence points to Poins instead of Peto having been with the Prince from the arrival of the Sheriff till the end of the play. Most modern editors have adopted this view, though some have not.

PURPOSE OF SCENE 3

1. To provide comic relief between two very serious scenes.

2. To bring the tavern characters into the main plot and link the two plots.

3. To give the audience a sense of the passage of time during

which the two armies have come together.

SUGGESTED QUESTIONS

1. What would you conclude about the Hostess' state of mind from her delightful speech in line 60, beginning, "Who, I?"?

2. Every time Falstaff calls the Hostess a decent name she contradicts him. Why does she do this?

ACT IV, SCENE 1

SYNOPSIS

The scene is laid in the rebel camp near Shrewsbury. To Hotspur, Worcester and Douglas, who are assembled, a messenger comes bringing letters from the Earl of Northumberland saying that he is ill and cannot come and he dare not turn over to anyone else the command of his forces. This is a severe blow, but Hotspur's resilient nature rises quickly to count it an advantage in two ways: they will have a force to fall back on if they are beaten at Shrewsbury, and their glory will be much the greater if they win.

Sir Richard Vernon, a recruit to their forces, joins them with the news that Westmoreland is approaching with seven thousand men and that the King is following with a larger army, that the Prince of Wales is coming, too, and that he and his officers look not only splendid but efficient. Furthermore, he has learned that Glendower cannot arrive for two weeks. This is the saddest blow of all, but Hotspur rises above it and prepares for action.

CHARACTERS IN SCENE 1

Hotspur

He and Douglas exchange compliments which sound exaggerated but which are genuine enough though clothed in the extravagant language of chivalry. He is very sarcastic about his father's illness, probably having had experience of such illness of his before, but his spirits rise again swiftly and he makes a virtue of necessity. He does not appreciate Vernon's promise of the Prince of Wales, because he has a fixed idea of him and cannot change it suddenly. The news of Glendower's delay is a tremendous blow, but he says he is confident they can do the job without him, though his reference to dying "merrily" indicates a slight sinking of heart.

Douglas

The bravest of the Scottish battle heroes of his time he deserves Hotspur's encomium. The fact that he mentions the Scottish disdain of the word "fear" does not disqualify him. Modern English restraint, reserve and understatement had not yet visited the world, and the language of mediaeval chivalry was full of this kind of talk, which the boaster as like as not would make good. In the battle later, he makes good.

Worcester

He knows his brother and is as suspicious as Hotspur is of the genuineness of the illness. His plans, he sees, are beginning to go awry. When the news about Glendower comes he would like to delay till Northumberland recovers, but he will not cross Hotspur's mood.

Vernon

An English country gentleman who has deserted from the royal forces to the Percys. He has actually been in the royal camp as is shown by his description of the Prince of Wales.

PURPOSE OF SCENE 1

1. To show the gradual deterioration of the rebel position of Northumberland and Glendower.

2. To show Hotspur's hot-headed, though courageous, over-confidence.

3. To give the audience an idea of the size of the royal army. We are not told the size of the rebel army, but by inference we gather it is not nearly as large.

ACT IV, SCENE 2

SYNOPSIS

On the way to Bridgenorth, Falstaff at the head of his company is passing near Coventry in Warwickshire. He will not march through Coventry because he is ashamed of the exceedingly ragged and disreputable company he leads. In a soliloquy he admits he has shamefully misused the King's commission to press or commandeer troops. He has sought out young men about to be married and all those who could buy themselves off and be left alone and has picked up only those dregs and unfortunates who had no money to buy themselves off with, and three hundred odd pounds for himself. In our values of today that would be nearly ten thousand dollars.

Hal is still in the mood to bait his old friend to obtain the inevitable Falstaffian reaction; in other words, he will be the supporting cast for a moment to see if the play is still going on each day. He finds it is. However, he has little time for it. The business ahead is too serious. He urges Falstaff on and departs.

Falstaff has made Bardolph his personal servant, or as we should say, his batman, and has sent him into Coventry for the invariable bottle of sack while he marches his sorry troops around outside the limits. We find that Peto has been made his lieutenant.

CHARACTERS IN SCENE 2

Falstaff

Quite unmoral, he has no cant or hypocrisy with himself. Nevertheless, his procedure is rascality. He has money enough now for himself, but none for his men who will have to steal their clothes from householders' washing hung out to dry. For the first time his daily one-act play by himself has a sinister tinge which Prince Hal notes. Of course, the Earl of Westmoreland not knowing Falstaff and never having come under his spell, is just plain scandalized at the look of these troops.

Prince Hal

He still appreciates the Falstaffian repartee and is willing to play supporting cast for a moment to give him his opportunity — but only for a moment. His business is too serious.

Bardolph

Now a corporal and Falstaff's batman. Apparently he carries his captain's current expense money.

PURPOSE OF SCENE 2

1. To furnish comic relief between two serious scenes.

2. To expose another facet of Falstaff's complex personality.

3. To keep the audience in touch with the royal army as it approaches Bridgenorth.

ACT IV, SCENE 3

SYNOPSIS

A dispute is staged in the rebel camp near Shrewsbury as to whether to attack at once that evening or to wait until the next day when men and horses which have just come in will be fresh. Hotspur and Douglas are all in favor of attacking at once; Worcester, backed by Vernon, is in favor of waiting until the next day. The point is settled for them by the arrival of Sir Walter Blunt with a request from the King to know the rebel complaints. The rebel leaders agree to talk it over and send an answer.

Sir Walter has refused to listen to Hotspur's long-winded account of the Percys' private pique and wants something more substantial. He returns to tell the King that the Earl of Worcester will go over to the royal camp early in the morning, if the King will send a hostage.

CHARACTERS IN SCENE 3

Hotspur

Again we see his impatience of delay and his preference for

action. Worcester's and Vernon's arguments seem wise but the audience cannot help but sympathize with Hotspur and at least half-believe that instant action may be the only salvation. Hotspur's charm asserts itself once more in his reception of Sir Walter Blunt and his very surprising acceptance of the invitation to send a message to the King.

Worcester

His natural caution appears clearly here. He is very sure of himself, and breaks out once in real alarm, "For God's sake, cousin."

Douglas

Like Hotspur, the man of instant action. He has not Hotspur's courtesy when he imputes cowardice to Vernon. He has no initiative of his own but backs up Hotspur at all times.

Vernon

Apparently a fine type of English country gentleman, even though he has deserted straight from the royal camp. Though his judgment is for delay till the next day, he will loyally follow Hotspur either that night or the next day.

Sir Walter Blunt

This time he appears to more advantage than before. He has a role to fill that gives him the opportunity to display some of his real character. He listens patiently to Hotspur's long tirade and recital of the Percys' private pique, but cuts it short when Hotspur stops to breathe. He has no defense to make for the King and must always be opposed to the rebels.

He is held in high esteem as we have seen before by the King. Now we see that he is held in high esteem by the rebels.

PURPOSE OF SCENE 3

1. To display the lack of unity in the counsels of the rebels.

2. To show King Henry's tact and caution toward the rebels;

also his determination that everyone shall know their case. It must be a clear-cut issue, and he knows that they may have difficulty in framing one for public consumption.

3. To show that most of the Percys' grievances are private piques.

SUGGESTED QUESTIONS

1. Line 88, "When he was personal in the Irish war." Express this in modern prose.

2. Line 97, "Disgraced me in my happy victories." How did Henry IV do this?

3. In line 103, what does Hotspur mean by, "this head of safety"?

ACT IV, SCENE 4

SYNOPSIS

In the Archbishop's palace at York the Archbishop is sending his retainer, Sir Michael, with letters to a number of his supporters in the rebellion. He is not optimistic of the outcome of the battle at Shrewsbury and is urging them to be prepared for an immediate visit from the King if he is successful. Sir Michael tries to take a more cheerful view, but the Archbishop remains apprehensive.

PURPOSE OF SCENE 4

1. To bring into definite focus the disparity of the royal army and the rebel forces.

2. To lead the audience to expect the defeat of the rebels.

3. To allow for time for the exchange of messengers between the two camps.

ACT V, SCENE 1

SYNOPSIS

The King, the Prince of Wales, Lord John of Lancaster, Sir Walter Blunt and Falstaff are appraising the probable weather for this day of battle. To them comes the Earl of Worcester with Vernon, bringing the rebel answer. Though the King shows his continued dislike of the Earl, he hears him patiently through the same long list of personal Percy grievances which the audience has heard so often before. There is no definite demand with this recital nor any national consideration.

The Prince of Wales interposes to offer to meet Hotspur in single combat to decide the issue and save lives. The King gives his approval.

The King adds that if they will depart to their homes there shall be a general amnesty for the rebels. The envoys leave.

The Prince remarks that neither offer will be accepted because Hotspur and Douglas together are too confident.

Alone with Falstaff, whom he has silenced when that irrepressible wag interrupted, he is besought by Falstaff for protection if Hal sees him down on the battlefield. The Prince advises him to say his prayers; he owes God a death.

Left alone, Falstaff goes into his famous soliloquy on honor. Honor cannot set a leg nor take away the pain from a wound, nor has it any skill in surgery. What is it? A word. Who has it? He that is dead. Does he feel it? No. Does it stay with the living? No. Why? Because envy will not allow it. So he will have none of it.

CHARACTERS IN SCENE 1

King Henry

He is dignified and self-possessed, assured and master of the situation. His offer of pardon is generous and he is obviously desirous of peace.

Prince Henry

The feature of his behavior is his gallantry and humility in his praise of Hotspur who has been so contemptuous of him. His offer of single combat is gallant, too, but he does not expect it to be taken up.

Worcester

His recital of the personal pique of his house is the final summing up of this theme. He asks for no specific remedy.

Falstaff

Even on the eve of the battle he cannot be serious; even in the royal presence. He humorously suggests to Prince Hal that he should act as squire to him if he sees him down. The Prince sees only the Falstaffian humor of it and the impossibility of anybody standing over him to protect him. His presence at the conference at all is a tribute to the Prince's good nature. As for his soliloquy on honor, if it is cynical, it is humorous. Perhaps one should remember that in hand-to-hand fighting, Falstaff was sure to be a sitting bird. A man of his girth, his age and lack of condition would have no more chance against an active young soldier than a dead man. He would not last a minute. There is some excuse for his attitude.

PURPOSE OF SCENE 1

1. To declare Prince Hal's challenge to Hotspur and show his admiration for Hotspur.

2. To show the King's patience in listening to the Percy story again and his generosity in offering amnesty to the rebels.

3. To show the King's calm command of the situation.

4. To bring Falstaff in at the end of the scene as comic relief between two serious scenes.

SUGGESTED QUESTIONS

1. What is the essential argument of Worcester's speech?

2. What considerations prompt Worcester and the Percys as far as the national welfare is concerned?

3. What considerations prompt Henry as far as the national welfare is concerned?

ACT V, SCENE 2

SYNOPSIS

Worcester overbears Vernon's opposition on the return to camp and gets him to promise to back him up in suppressing the report of the King's offer of general pardon. Worcester simply tells Hotspur that the King intends to attack the rebels shortly. Hotspur sends defiance back to the royal camp by the Earl of Westmoreland who has been a hostage while the Earl of Worcester was in the royal camp. Worcester, lying, says that the King promised to scourge the Percys as rebels and traitors. He then tells Hotspur of the Prince of Wales' challenge. Hotspur is curious to know how he bore himself when delivering it. Vernon interposes and delivers a splendid eulogy of the Prince. Hotspur says he intends to meet him on the field. He calls his forces to arms.

Messengers arrive with letters probably from the Archbishop, but Hotspur is too busy to bother with them. Another messenger comes in to say that the royal army is moving forward, and Hotspur goes out to battle.

CHARACTERS IN SCENE 2

Worcester

Here he finally shows his full hand as the treacherous conspirator, treacherous even to his own nephew. It is plain that he fears for his plans and for his own skin and does not care for anybody else's.

Vernon

As a newcomer and a junior, he bows to Worcester's treacherous decision, but as a gentleman he tells the truth about Prince Hal and gives such a glowing picture of him that Hotspur says he must be in love with the Prince.

Hotspur

He would not have Worcester beg mercy from the King; that is the Percy pride. He would like to meet the Prince of Wales in personal combat and will try to do so during the battle. He is much too impatient to bother with letters at such a time. Besides, he knows no letter can interfere with the result now. As military commander, he orders the freeing of Westmoreland and the beginning of the battle.

PURPOSE OF SCENE 2

1. It sets forth the Earl of Worcester's treachery unmistakably.

2. It shows the battle beginning.

ACT V, SCENE 3

SYNOPSIS

These short battle scenes are divided into episodes. There are three such in this scene: between Douglas and Sir Walter Blunt, Hotspur's conversation with Douglas, and the Prince's conversation with Falstaff.

1. Douglas meets Sir Walter Blunt who is masquerading as the King. They fight and Douglas kills Blunt, thinking he has killed the King.

2. Hotspur appears and compliments Douglas, who is elated over his victory over the King. Hotspur recognizes Sir Walter Blunt, and tells Douglas that the King has many wearing his royal coat. Douglas, furious, vows that he will

murder the whole royal wardrobe till he meets the King.

3. Falstaff, alone, comes upon Sir Walter Blunt lying dead and soliloquizes, "There's honour for you." His company has been killed off except for three who have fled the field. His is concerned to keep his own life. He cannot be serious about his own life or Sir Walter's even in the midst of a battle in which his own chances are slim indeed, being the mark he is. Critics have been severe upon him in this scene and have talked of his callousness and cynicism. Neither epithet really applies. He is just playing his play.

The Prince of Wales comes upon him and wants to borrow his sword. When Falstaff hears that Hotspur is still very much alive, he refuses to lend his sword. When the Prince tries to borrow his pistol, he finds the holster filled with a bottle of sack, which, in disgust, he throws at Falstaff's head and rushes away.

Falstaff soliloquizes, "Give me life: which, if I can save, so; if not, honour comes unlooked for, and there's an end."

The truth is, and most critics have not realized this though Falstaff did full well, that he had no business being on that battlefield in the first place.

CHARACTERS IN SCENE 3

Sir Walter Blunt
This loyal old knight, tried and trusted friend of the King, meets his death protecting that King by wearing his royal insignia.

Douglas
A fearless fighter, he makes good his boast of the evening before.

Prince Hal
Fighting furiously, he has lost or broken his sword. He does not care where he gets another so long as he has one in his hand. He knows that he can use it better than Falstaff can, but we can

certainly see Falstaff's point of view. He is furious with Falstaff when he finds no pistol but a bottle of sack in his holster, because he is disappointed of a weapon, not because he is disappointed in Falstaff.

Falstaff
    His character has been discussed in the above synopsis.

PURPOSE OF SCENE 3

1. To keep the audience in suspense by showing an initial ascendancy of the rebel forces.

2. To provide a comic relief between two serious episodes.

3. To show the mood of Prince Hal in action.

ACT V, SCENE 4

SYNOPSIS

In this scene there are five episodes. The rebels lose their advantage and the royal cause prevails.

Episode 1.—King Henry, the Prince of Wales, Prince John, and the Earl of Westmoreland.

The Prince of Wales is slightly wounded and the King urges him to retire to have his wound dressed, sending Prince John with him. Prince John flatly refuses to go unless he is wounded too. The Prince urges the King to show himself in the battleline for fear they will think he has left the field. The King sends Westmoreland with Prince Hal, who refuses to bother with his wound. Prince John calls to Westmoreland and they rush off to a part of the field where they are needed. Prince Hal is struck with admiration for his younger brother's spirit and rushes out into action.

Episode 2.—The King, left alone, is attacked by Douglas, who is on the point of overwhelming him, when he is saved by Prince Hal, who beats Douglas off. The King is grateful, and is delighted to find that instead of wishing for his death his son saves his life. He goes forward into the field.

Episode 3. — As soon as the King is gone Hotspur rushes in, recognizes the Prince, gives his own name, and they fight. Falstaff comes in and cheers Prince Hal on for all the world like a modern football "rooter."

Douglas comes in and engages Falstaff, who, recognizing swiftly that he has no chance, falls as though hit and shams death. Douglas, too busy to bother paying further attention to him, rushes out.

Hotspur is run through, apparently in the visor, and falls dying. As he lies dying he regrets the loss of his proud titles of glory. Even in death his high poetic phraseology will not be denied and he does some memorable lines.

Prince Hal bends over him, opens his visor, and does him the courtesy of covering his mangled face with his scarf. Then he notices Falstaff, thinks he is dead, and says farewell in terms of fondness. He promises to see later that he is disemboweled for embalming, and goes out.

Episode 4. — Falstaff, who has heard all this, is especially shaken by the Prince's last remarks about disemboweling. As soon as the Prince is gone he rises unsteadily to his feet and says that, if the Prince disembowels him, he will give him leave to eat him with pepper and salt the next day. He soliloquizes on the rightness of his action in counterfeiting death. He notices Hotspur lying dead, and the thought strikes him that he may be counterfeiting too. So he makes sure he is dead by running him through again with his sword, this time in his thigh. Then he has the idea of claiming to have killed him. So he hoists him on his back (quite a feat with a corpse in full armor) and staggers off with him.

Episode 5. — Staggering along with the corpse of Hotspur on his back, he runs straight into the Prince of Wales and his brother, Prince John. The battle is over and won and they are making a survey of the field. Prince Hal cannot believe his eyes, because he is certain he saw Falstaff quite dead. Falstaff throws down Hotspur's corpse, claims to have killed him and expects to be made a duke or an earl. The Prince knows that he killed Hotspur by a wound through the face, but Falstaff says that they both got to their feet and fought an hour by Shrewsbury clock. The Prince will not dispute it. He knows that Falstaff is lying and tells him so, but the consciousness of having done the thing is enough for him. Falstaff can have what credit he can get out of it.

CHARACTERS IN SCENE 4

Prince Hal

His conduct is fearless and energetic in the battle. His defense of his father at the moment of dire need sets his father's mind at rest about his character. Generous in his unenvious praise of his brother's prowess, he is generous, too, in his attitude toward Hotspur. Too great-souled to be worried about Falstaff's lying pretensions to victory over Hotspur, he does not cast him off. He shows clearly that he has redeemed his earlier promises to himself and to his father.

King Henry

In actual battle action his leadership begins to diminish as that of the Prince of Wales increases. Still he is the King, though we do not see his command displayed as in the council-room.

Hotspur

He makes a mistake in despising the Prince of Wales when he engages him. He cannot rid his mind of the idea that he has formed of him from hearsay. His death is a great surprise and blow to him, not that he fears death, but he cannot bring himself to believe it possible from such a hand. Of course, it is nonsense to speak of his proud titles passing to Prince Hal. They were his forever.

Douglas

That he retreats when Prince Hal rescues his father is nothing against him. He is now hopelessly out-matched, one against two, one almost as good as he—the King, one a little better—the Prince. There is other work for him to do on the battlefield. That he goes away after laying out Falstaff is perfectly natural. Time presses, and he is needed in many places. He thoroughly redeems his boastful language of the evening before which, after all, was a commonplace of the days of chivalry.

Falstaff

Even in his dire peril and on the battlefield he can play his play and a bright and humorous thing it is. Even his rascality with regard to Hotspur, and his ghoulish stab into a dead body, have a grotesque humor of their own. The laughable absurdity of his claim to have mastered Hotspur seems to tickle the Prince in spite of himself.

SUGGESTED QUESTIONS

1. Write out a brief connected resume of Falstaff's argument concerning counterfeiting, line 111.

2. What ignominy does Prince Hal refer to in line 100?

3. What does the King mean to say in line 48 by, "Thou hast redeemed thy lost opinion"?

4. What is Hal's meaning in line 57, "And saved the treacherous labour of your son"?

ACT V, SCENE 5

SYNOPSIS

The battle is over and the royal cause victorious. The Earl of Worcester and Sir Richard Vernon are brought in prisoners before the King, who bitterly upbraids Worcester for having suppressed part of the message he was charged with to Hotspur. The King sends both the prisoners to be summarily executed. He says that he will review the cases of the other leaders.

Prince Hal reports that the Earl of Douglas is in his tent a prisoner, all bruised from having fallen over a low precipice in his flight. He begs to be allowed to dispose of him, which request his father instantly grants. Thereupon Prince Hal turns to his brother John and gives him the commission of going to his tent and setting the Earl of Douglas free without ransom as a token of their admiration for his valor that day.

The King divides his forces. Westmoreland with Prince John will proceed toward York to deal with the Archbishop of York and the Earl of Northumberland. He himself with the Prince of Wales will proceed against Glendower and Mortimer, Earl of March.

CHARACTERS IN SCENE 5

King Henry

He resumes his kingly place as master of the war. His sentencing of Worcester and Vernon to death is because they betrayed their trust as messengers and caused an unnecessary battle, not because they were in arms against him. His further lenience is foreshadowed. His delivery of the Earl of Douglas to the Prince of Wales is part of his lenience, because undoubtedly he understands what the Prince intends to do with him.

Prince Hal

He shows his magnanimity in releasing Douglas without ransom, and more than that his unselfish admiration of excellence in others, even enemies.

SUMMARIES OF LEADING CHARACTERS

King Henry

Apart from what his words and actions in the play reveal of his character, this is clearly drawn by himself in his exhortation to the Prince of Wales and by his enemies, the Percys. We see a man of boldness and quick decision, prompt to act and with no misgivings, one who plans subtly and far in advance of the event, and who where once started on a course follows the steps of that course with machine-like precision, never looking back. Cold he is in nature, calculating and not lovable. Always master of himself, always master of the situation, he has the power from this to bend all sorts of other men to his purpose till he needs them no more and they are helpless against him. Not that he throws them away, nor does he kick down the ladder by which they climbed, but he insists that they remain in the sphere he has assigned them and subservient to his will.

Though there is no patriotic shouting from the King's side throughout the play the inference is, and it would strike all Englishmen of Shakespeare's day automatically, that Henry IV was on the side of a united country of England and Wales, and that it would have been a disaster of the first magnitude if the rebels had won and split the country into three.

The Prince of Wales

Here for once in literature there is a plausible, an entirely believable change in character shown before our eyes on the stage, and the reason is that the elements of the fine and noble leader were there in the background of what appeared to be an idler and a waster. His true nature is revealed by a subtle almost unnoticeable development from scene to scene, and at no time do we feel that there is anything ignoble, anything base about him. It is Falstaff who is the magnet and it is wit, not sack nor women nor robbing travellers which are his pre-occupation. In other words, Sir John Falstaff is a mental stimulus of a remarkable order and his humor, his geniality, his expansive human fellowship are what fascinate the Prince. Why should he seek the company of this rather disreputable knight rather than find an outlet for his energy at court? Because there was not, nor could there be, anything there — no company nor group — half so exhilarating.

When there is responsibility and noble action to call him he responds with alacrity, for the underlying stuff is there; in fact it is hardly underlying; it shows through.

A singularly modest and generous personality, he is unaffected at all times, and his words and actions very direct.

Prince John

He is introduced here because he is to be important in the plays that follow in the sequence, *Henry V* and *Henry VI*. The one real glimpse we get of him is on the battle-field at Shrewsbury when he refuses to obey his father and conduct Prince Hal to his tent unless he is wounded too. Also when, in company with his brother, he comes face to face with Falstaff lugging the corpse of Hotspur on his back. No wonder he exclaims, "This is the strangest tale that ever I heard." He did not know Falstaff.

The Earl of Westmoreland

Brother-in-law to the King through Henry's half-sister, he is loyal throughout the reign. He is the King's chief adviser and executive. He is in charge of arrangements for the crusade at the beginning of the play, he is Henry's chief general during the rising, though we see him only once for a moment with Prince John during the episodes of battle action. A capable trusted senior officer.

Sir Walter Blunt

A highly respected, loyal old knight, trusted as a messenger, and it is as a messenger that he appears throughout the play till the last act. The longest speech we have from him is when he delivers the King's message in the rebel camp. It is direct and concise. He cannot be fooled and abruptly shuts Hotspur up when he has stood all he can of Hotspur's rhetoric. He meets his death at the hands of Douglas because he is protecting his King by wearing his insignia.

The Earl of Worcester

A crafty, scheming man he is the villain of the piece. Brother of the Earl of Northumberland and uncle of Hotspur, he has that fierce family pride which binds these Percys together. It is he who initiates the plot for the rising. In fact, he has the thing already under way when he first mentions it to Hotspur when he is so wrought up against the King. He is dismissed from the council chamber by the King for his insolence of word, look and bearing. His grand theme is the ingratitude of the King to the Percys who have helped him to the throne. He is shrewd, and wise and experienced in the ways of men. He tries to temper the impatience and impetuosity of his famous nephew, and has some influence on him, though it is temporary. His great treachery, for which he is executed, is the suppression of the mention of the King's offer of pardon to the rebel army.

The Earl of Northumberland

He appears in the play first as a smooth and plausible peace-maker between the king and his son, Hotspur, urging very doubtful considerations. When the King leaves he adopts his brother Worcester's plan for a rising, but cautiously, when the time comes for action to aid his son, he chooses to be ill and to allow no one else to raise his troops or lead those he has raised on the specious excuse of fearing to incriminate such a person. At the end of the last act we see the King about to send Westmoreland to deal with him anyway.

Hotspur

A man who has already made a great name for himself as a mighty and chivalrous warrior. Charged with the defense of the northern border of England his enemies have been chiefly Scots. His obsession is honor and by that he means chiefly prowess in battle, but he would also add absence of all unfairness, meanness or bitterness. His is a rough but generous nature. He has little manners and no delicacy. He has a sense of humor tending to caprice and derision. His rough passionate soul is capable of great flights of poetic expression, forced out of him by the vehemence of his nature. Yet he despises writers and singers of poetry. He will not make it an object; it simply comes naturally to him as a medicine. He is capable of great tenderness too, as to his wife, but it finds expression in a certain capricious roughness, as though he were ashamed of it as tending to ruin his warrior's hardness. Impetuous, impatient, uncontrolled and uncontrollable he is a dominating and domineering personality amongst all his social equals and subordinates.

Edmund Mortimer, Earl of March

With a better claim to the throne than Henry IV, he had never thought of deposing Richard and so short circuiting the succession. This is what Henry did. Mortimer was not the man to do it, in any case.

His claim came from the fact that he was descended from an elder son of Edward III's than John of Gaunt who was Henry's father. Also Richard had designated him his heir, though there was nothing legally binding in that. We get only one glimpse of him in the play, and it is not reassuring. He is not the type suited for generalship or kingship especially in those days of great territorial lords who chafed at any interference from the King. He disgusted Hotspur with his sentimentality towards his bride in public. Hotspur was trying to make him king because he was his wife's brother.

The Archbishop of York

Mentioned several times as an astute prelate, and of course, great baron, he approves the plot, and is up to his ears in it. We get only a glimpse of him and then he is trying to mend his forces in great panic. If the rebels lose the battle of Shrewsbury, he expects a visitation from the King in force. The last we hear of him is Henry giving orders for that visitation to take place.
take place.

Archibald, Earl of Douglas

He has a great reputation as a fighter on the southern Scottish border, yet he has been defeated by Hotspur three times and captured the last time. He is a fearless, doughty fighter, but boastful as many of his class tended to be at the time. He wins the admiration not only of Hotspur, but of the Prince of Wales also, who as Hotspur did before, sets him free without ransom.

Owen Glendower

Leader in a Welsh revolt — or series of revolts — against not only the King, but the English in general. He is credited with great magical powers, and he seems to have believed it himself, though not above chicanery at times. An educated and accomplished man, he is externally far more of a gentleman than Hotspur. The latter would for his own arrogant whim break up the alliance. Glendower would not be willing to do so. In spite of the pretensions he is a likable not to say charming personality, and a first class guerilla leader in war.

Sir Richard Vernon

An English country gentleman of Chishire who had never

really acquiesced in Henry's seizure of the throne. A fine type, who describes the Prince of Wales in glowing terms. He was in the camp before Vernon arrived with the rebels and later when the Prince delivered his challenge to single combat. His serious mistake, for which he is executed, is in yielding to Worcester and concealing the King's offer of pardon to the rebel army.

Sir John Falstaff

The most humorous character, probably, ever created in literature. He lives in a world of extraordinary make-believe, yet he is very practical and knows this hard-knock world of reality very well. He tells the most egregious lies, but he does not expect them to be believed. The truth is, he is forever playing a play on an imaginary stage and he is always the center of the stage. Every minute of every day he is playing one. He has the power—and it is sheer mental fascination that does it—of impressing anyone and everyone he meets into a supporting role in a supporting cast whose duty it is to feed him opportunities to display his amazing effortless nimbleness of wit. If he cannot find a supporting cast, an audience will do until he can turn it into a supporting cast, as he is bound to do sooner or later. And if he seems abusive at times he does not expect anyone to believe the abuse, and he turns it on himself as often as on anyone else.

His fascination is largely that he is on such good terms with the world in general and has such overflowing good nature toward all about him. Throughout a day, he hardly spends a dozen serious words and he must have his jest in a highway-robbery, in the presence of the King during an audience, on the field of battle; it matters not where. It is all the pure joy of the exercise of his amazingly versatile wit.

He is no coward though he does things that we would call cowardly. He is no cynic, though he says and does things that might be termed cynical. He is an extraordinary mixture and contradiction of natures, but the key to his character is make-believe.

Poins

He seems to be even more an intimate of the Prince's than

Falstaff but certainly takes second place to him. They seem to be of an age or there abouts and also seem to have other relationships which are outside the sphere of the Boar's Head Inn. Poins probably introduced the Prince to this society, and certain it is that Falstaff seems to like him and says so even when he is suffering at his hands the night of the robbery. He cooked up the plot against Falstaff and carried out the details. He flies off the handle at Falstaff at the word coward, but the Prince accepts it serenely, probably understanding Falstaff better. There is good reason to believe that Peto's name was substituted for Poins by typographical error.

Gadshill
Rather an ordinary professional confederate, an arranger for professional highwaymen.

Peto
An associate of the thieves, he first appears at the robbery. At the end of the play he turns up as Falstaff's lieutenant.

Bardolph
The blazing carbuncles on his nose and cheeks, the result of steady drinking, are his outstanding feature. These serve as a butt for both Prince Hal and Falstaff, but we find at least that he is sensitive about them. The Prince uses him as messenger and he ends up in this play as a corporal and Falstaff's batman.

Lady Percy
Historically, her name was Elizabeth, but one did not use the name Elizabeth on the English stage in 1597. Shakespeare seemed to have a fondness for the name Kate and it suits the wife of Hotspur better. Madly in love with her husband she understands his every mood and falls in with each automatically. But she can discipline him, in his own language too, if she avoids the slight show of serious sentiment in public; witness the scene in the Archdeacons house at Bangor.

Lady Mortimer
A lovely spoiled girl whose interests are music and love, and she's very much in love now. Anyway she is on her honeymoon.

She insists on having her own way and going to the war with Mortimer, and her father can do nothing with her. She dissolves in tears when she is crossed. She serves to make it plain in this scene that Mortimer is not the stuff for kingship.

Mistress Quickly, The Hostess

There are two scenes in which she figures here. She is an old acquaintance of Sir John Falstaff's and has been very generous to him in the past. She is fascinated by him, as she shows in the extempore play scene. In the other scene, Falstaff playfully stands her mentally on her head and then whirls her round till she is raging. Yet the moment he beams on her and speaks sweetly in language she can follow, she is his meek, adoring servant again and runs to get the breakfast for him that he will never pay for.

GENERAL NOTES

THE NAME FALSTAFF

In Act I, Scene 2, line 40 occurs the puzzling remark of Prince Hal's, "My old lad of the castle," referring to Falstaff. This is the sole remaining trace (a careless oversight in preparing the manuscript for the press) of the original name of the Falstaffian character — Sir John Oldcastle. The original Sir John Oldcastle, Lord Cobham, a very real person, was a well-known Lollard who was burned at the stake in Henry IV's reign. After his death his name and character were ridiculed by his enemies and his name became a popular synonym for profligacy and gluttony. His name was connected with that of Prince Henry in popular legend and he was commonly regarded as the Prince's corrupter. Early in the seventeenth century a movement, led by the real Sir John Oldcastle's descendants and backed by Puritan influence, came to a head. Its purpose was to vindicate the memory of the martyr. On this account, Shakespeare changed the name to Falstaff. He was bitterly assailed for this name too, because there was a historical character named Sir John Fastolf, who also was a Lollard, and a distinguished person in the war in France in Henry VI's reign. It was objected by his descendants and admirers that Falstaff was a thin disguise for the name Fastolf, but the strongest protest came after Shakespeare's death and no further change was made.

CONFUSION OF NAME MORTIMER

In Act III, Scene 1, line 196, occurs, "she and my aunt Percy shall follow." This shows the confusion in the historian Holinshed's mind about the Mortimers, and Shakespeare followed Holinshed's chronicle. The Mortimer who married Glendower's daughter was indeed the brother of Hotspur's wife, but he was the uncle of the Mortimer who was Earl of March. The latter was about ten years old at the time of the events of the play and was kept securely confined by King Henry in Windsor Castle.

ARRAS

The walls of the mediaeval castles were cold bare stone and perpetually damp. The practice grew up of covering them (and the doors and doorways to prevent drafts) with heavy drapes having brightly colored pictures woven into them. These were hung some distance out from the walls to prevent the damp rotting the fabric. This became a fashion and spread far beyond the great stone castles. Practically all the original drapes of this type were woven in the town of Arras in France, well-known to Canadian troops in the first Great War. Hence the name arras. There was plenty of standing room in most cases between these drapes and the wall and countless plays of the Elizabethan period used this device of concealment behind the arras.

AGE OF PRINCE HALAM HOTSPUR

Historically Prince Hal was sixteen and Hotspur thirty-eight at the time of the battle of Shrewsbury. King Henry IV was only thirty-six. For dramatic effect Shakespeare equalizes the age of Prince Hal and Hotspur and adds years to that of Henry IV.

SWEARING, BIBLICAL QUOTATIONS

By an act passed in 1603, the year of James I's accession, it was forbidden to actors in theaters to swear, use the name of the diety or use Biblical quotations on the stage. Fortunately, the full text has survived in the published versions. Falstaff uses more Biblical quotations than any others of Shakespeare's characters, and never irreverently. Nor is there any offensive allusion to Puritans in this play.

LORD MORTIMER OF SCOTLAND

In Act III, Scene 2, line 164, Sir Walter Blunt mentions Lord Mortimer of Scotland. This is another confusion, this time with the name March. The person intended was George Dunbar, Earl of March in the Scottish peerage.

LIME IN SACK

Falstaff complains that his sherry is adulterated with lime. It was a trick of the trade for vintners at times to put lime in wine that was stale or flat to make it sparkle and give it life.

THE USE OF PROSE AND POETRY

Blank verse, that is unrhymed, iambic pentameter was the normal vehicle for Shakespeare's plays, but in *Henry IV* only a little more than half the lines are in blank verse. The rest are prose. Blank verse is always used for the speeches of the principal characters and nobility, except when they are associating with more ordinary ranks of society. It is used to carry on the main stream of the story.

Prose is used for anything extraneous, letters, or persons speaking out of their natural character. It is used for the speech of those of lower social standing than the main characters, and for all humorous scenes.

Rhyme is rarely used: mainly in couplets to mark the end of a scene. There is very little rhyme in *Henry IV*. It was Shakespeare's tendency to use it less and less as he grew older. There are only 42 such rhyming couplets in the play.

DRAMATIC CONSTRUCTION IN HENRY IV

In both tragedy and comedy there are five stages of plot development.

1. **The exposition** or explanation or introduction: Act I, Scene 1, to Act I, Scene 3.

2. **The complication** or rising action: Act I, Scene 3, 124-302, to Act II, Scene 4.

3. **The climax**, or crisis or turning point: Act III, Scene 1.

4. **The resolution**, falling action or consequence: Act III, Scene 2, to Act V, Scene 3.

5. **The denouement** or conclusion: Act V, Scene 4, to Act V, Scene 5.

THE DURATION OF THE ACTION

Historic time is the period between June 22, 1402, when Mortimer was taken prisoner by Glendower and the battle of Shrewsbury, July 21, 1403.

The dramatic time is ten main or history days and three Falstaffian days with their intervals, a total stretch of about three months.

SOLILOQUIES

1. Act I, Scene 2, line 197 – Prince of Wales: "I know you all –"

2. Act II, Scene 2, line 10 – Falstaff: "I am accurs'd to rob –"

3. Act II, Scene 3, line 1 – Hotspur (reading letter).

4. Act III, Scene 3, line 205 — Falstaff: "Rare words! — "

5. Act IV, Scene 2, line 11 — Falstaff: "If I be not ashamed of my soldiers — "

6. Act V, Scene 1, line 127 — Falstaff: " 'Tis not due yet — "

7. Act V, Scene 3, line 57 — Falstaff: "Well, if Percy be alive — "

8. Act V, Scene 4, line 111 — Falstaff: "Emboweled! if thou embowel me — "

9. Act V, Scene 4, line 161 — Falstaff: "I'll follow, as they say, for reward."

A soliloquy is a device of the dramatist to enable the audience to share the inmost thoughts, feelings and intentions of the character on the stage. The character speaks aloud to himself and unburdens his whole mind or soul. Although people do speak aloud to themselves often enough, and it was a very convenient and time-saving device to dramatists of former days, for the last sixty years or more our audiences and therefore our dramatists will have none of it.

QUESTIONS AND ANSWERS

1. *Question:*

Compare the characters of Hotspur and Glendower so far as they are revealed in the scene at Bangor or where the indentures are drawn up.

Answer:

Glendower, of poetic temperament, superstitious belief, and vast conceit has pretensions to magical powers. He is interested in the supernatural as exemplified in early Welsh history, and thinks every one else should be. On the other hand, he is, at least externally, far more of a gentleman than Hotspur. He is far more prudent, for he will not endanger the alliance by a hasty word or by personal pique. His relation to poetry is this, that he regards it as a sufficient end in itself. Hotspur does not. He is courageous, but not impetuously rash.

Hotspur is not superstitious; he despises superstition. He has nothing but contempt for Glendower's claims to magic powers. The relation of the ancient Welsh tales with their atmosphere of the supernatural bores him to tears. He is naturally poetic but it is the unforced, automatic expression of his fervent and impetuous nature pressed out of him by his fiery, headlong spirit. His manners are rough, and he is arrogant. To dominate the council he will risk the whole alliance. Yet, he can be generous and agreeable. The moment Glendower drops his peremptory denial of the proposition regarding the Trent, he drops his. He is obviously in love with Lady Percy, but his contempt for sentiment, or sentimentality in public, expresses itself in derisive mockery. He is downright blunt where Glendower is courteous and polished. His masterfulness will endure no opposition, his impatience no delay. Glendower has been used to domination too, but he will defer when he sees the need, and he will not rush into action without being sure the time is propitious.

2. **Question:**
   Explain—"And will awhile uphold the unyoked humour of your idleness."

   Answer:
   I will be your companion for awhile in this carefree, irresponsible life. Prince Hal has no intention of leaving this irresponsible life yet.

3. **Question:**
   Explain—"I better brook the loss of brittle life than those proud titles thou hast won of me."

   Answer:
   Hotspur does not fear death, but he is laboring under the delusion that the glory of his past achievements will now

accrue to Prince Hal. This, of course, is absurd. His glory was and is forever his own.

4. *Question:*

How does Shakespeare make the meeting of the rebels in Bangor interesting?

Answer:

By the presentation of the furious clash of two such opposite and head-strong temperaments as those of Hotspur and Glendower. Also by the introduction of the two ladies who are as contrasting in character and temperament as Hotspur and Glendower, and the relief of an interesting domestic scene with its derisive mimicry on Hotspur's part.

5. *Question:*

What grievances had Mistress Quickly against Falstaff?

Answer:

She accused him of owing her for a dozen shirts which she bought for him; of owing twenty-four pounds which she lent him; and of owing a large bill for meals and another for drinks between meals.

6. *Question:*

Write in your own words Prince Hal's defense of his association with rogues.

Answer:

He will continue to consort with these low companions and will endure the disappointment and disapprobation of people at large for awhile so that when he does emerge their astonishment will be so great and their expectations so confounded that he will shine doubly bright by contrast with the life they have thought him leading.

7. *Question:*

What leads Worcester to conceal Henry's offer of pardon?

Answer:

He tells Vernon that he distrusts the King's word; that the King might forgive Hotspur on account of his youth and fame, but sooner or later he would take vengeance under cover of some other offense on Northumberland and himself. Reading between the lines (or listening) we can see that he cannot bear to see his painfully built-up plot go awry and he himself be relegated to a corner. He still has hope that Hotspur and Douglas may lead the rebel forces to victory.

8. *Question:*

What characteristics of Hotspur are shown in Scene III?

Answer:

He shows courtesy in his speech to the King, a quality of vivid imagination and high poetic diction, an obstinacy when he contradicts the King about Mortimer, and a fiery temper, ill-suppressed. He shows as well a clannish feeling in his concern for and upholding of Mortimer who is his wife's brother.

When the King leaves, the flood-gates of his passion are unlocked, and he becomes derisive, abusive, passionate. He is uncontrolled and uncontrollable, utterly impatient and impetuous. However, when he does listen, his mind is quick to seize the implications of the plot and to adopt it with headlong enthusiasm.

9. *Question:*

How did the rebels propose to divide England?

Answer:

All west of the Severn to be ruled by Glendower; all north of the Trent to be ruled by the Percys; all south and east of the Trent and the Severn to be ruled by Mortimer.

10. *Question:*

Who delivers the closing speech of the play? What instructions are issued in it? What purpose is served by this speech?

Answer:
King Henry delivers the speech.

Westmoreland and Prince John are to lead their army to investigate the activities of the Archbishop of York and of Northumberland. He himself with the Prince of Wales will proceed against Glendower and Mortimer.

The purpose served is to put an effective end to the recent action and the play, and to point forward to future action in another play.

NOTES

NOTES